This project is promoted by
INTESA [m] SANPAOLO
as part of Progetto Cultura

Concept and supervision

Art, Culture and Historical Heritage
Executive Director
Gallerie d'Italia
Director
Michele Coppola

Promotion, Marketing and Cultural Partnerships
Laurence Aliquot

Promotion and Cultural Marketing
Simona Cantone

Publishing and Music Coordination
Project Manager
Rosanna Benedini

Editing
Valeria Tortosa

Graphic Design
Zelda was a writer

Copy-editing
Arianna Ghilardotti

Layout
Alessandro Minoggi

Iconographic Research
Paola Lamanna

Translations
Patricia Garvin

The illustrations and the cover
by Zelda was a writer are published
in agreement with MalaTesta Lit. Ag. Milan

Special thanks to Civita Mostra e Musei
for sharing the project's educational objectives.

First published in Italy in 2021 by
Skira editore S.p.A.
Palazzo Casati Stampa
via Torino 61
20123 Milano
Italy
www.skira.net

© 2021 Intesa Sanpaolo
© 2021 Skira editore

All rights reserved under international copyright conventions.
No part of this book may be reproduced or utilised in any form or by any means, electronic or mechanical, including photocopying, recording, or any information storage and retrieval system, without permission in writing from the publisher.

Printed and bound in Italy. First edition

ISBN: 978-88-572-4668-0

Distributed in USA, Canada, Central & South America by ARTBOOK | D.A.P., 75 Broad Street, Suite 630, New York, NY 10004, USA.
Distributed elsewhere in the world by Thames and Hudson Ltd., 181A High Holborn, London WC1V 7QX, United Kingdom.

texts
STEFANO ZUFFI

edited by
MARTINA FUGA

ON A MISSION in... ITALY

illustrations: ZELDA WAS A WRITER

Edizioni Gallerie d'Italia | Skira

On a mission in... Italy is a journey to discover Italy and its wonders by following the stages of the Grand Tour, a journey through Italy young eighteenth-century Europeans took to develop their cultural knowledge.
This journey involves 10 missions you will undertake with an exceptional guide: Johann Wolfgang von Goethe – "Wolfy" to his friends.

Wolfy was a writer, poet, and philosopher, an enthusiastic, multitalented man, who at the age of 37 set off on his first tour of Italy, a trip that lasted almost two years.
He described it in his book *Italian Journey*, a major bestseller. What better guide could you have on this adventure?

Pack pens, pencils, scissors, colours, an eraser, glue, a pinch of curiosity and a great desire to explore and discover new things.

have a good trip!

THE FIRST "TOURISTS"

About three hundred years ago, at the beginning of the eighteenth century, the custom began among young and wealthy intellectuals from central and northern Europe of "taking a Grand Tour", a long journey that might even last several years, with Italy as its principal destination. Since then, travellers looking for a complete cultural, artistic and historical education have been called "tourists".

Before the arrival of tourists, major Italian cities renowned for their artistic heritage were visited by the likes of painters, sculptors and architects, musicians, poets and writers, who came to Italy to explore the latest in the arts and literature. Venice, Florence, and especially Rome welcomed more and more numerous groups, who besides visiting the masterpieces of the past were especially attracted by the chance of meeting famous people and of personally experiencing the latest styles and trends. Even so, the main point of a visit to Italy was to take a journey through history.

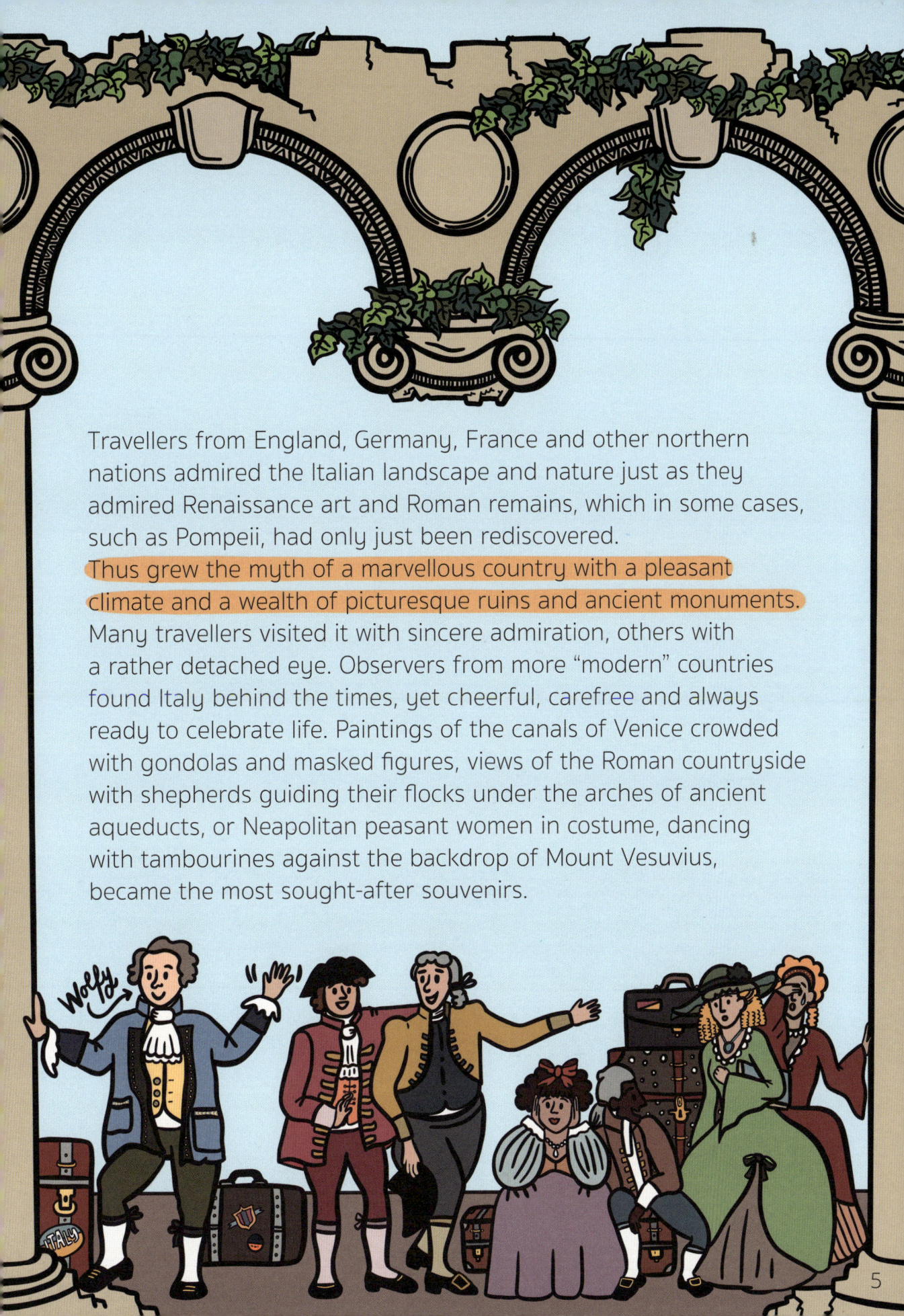

Travellers from England, Germany, France and other northern nations admired the Italian landscape and nature just as they admired Renaissance art and Roman remains, which in some cases, such as Pompeii, had only just been rediscovered. Thus grew the myth of a marvellous country with a pleasant climate and a wealth of picturesque ruins and ancient monuments. Many travellers visited it with sincere admiration, others with a rather detached eye. Observers from more "modern" countries found Italy behind the times, yet cheerful, carefree and always ready to celebrate life. Paintings of the canals of Venice crowded with gondolas and masked figures, views of the Roman countryside with shepherds guiding their flocks under the arches of ancient aqueducts, or Neapolitan peasant women in costume, dancing with tambourines against the backdrop of Mount Vesuvius, became the most sought-after souvenirs.

MISSION 1

Here are the stages of the Grand Tour that the first tourists thought were unmissable. Add the name of your own town or city, or a place in Italy you've already visited or would like to include in your itinerary.

Now it's your turn! Glue a photo of your town and write some travel tips for tourists who visit it.

MY TOWN

name: _____
_____
where is it? _____
_____
_____
when to visit it: _____
_____

10 THINGS to SEE

1. _____
2. _____
3. _____
4. _____
5. _____
6. _____
7. _____
8. _____
9. _____
10. _____

5 THINGS to EAT

1) _____
2) _____
3) _____
4) _____
5) _____

ITALY: WONDERFUL ...BUT COMPLICATED

At the time of the Grand Tour, Italy as a nation did not yet exist, or more precisely its territory was divided into many different states.

Those who crossed the Brenner Pass and reached Lake Garda entered the lands of the Most Serene Republic of Venice, whereas those who came from the Simplon or the Gotthard Pass and descended toward the sparkling waters of Lake Maggiore or Lake Como, entered the former Duchy of Milan, which had then become part of the Austrian Empire. From city to city, travellers passed through numerous borders, customs and controls, with continual changes in systems of measurement and currency. Thalers, ducats, florins, lire and scudi; gold, silver, bronze and copper coins: travelling in Italy meant getting used to ever-changing currencies – and making quick calculations to avoid being cheated!

After their laborious journey through the Alpine passes, European travellers looking out towards the lakes felt they had arrived in an enchanted place full of antiquities, music, and art, and resplendent with gardens and sunshine.
From Venice to Florence and from Rome to Naples and Sicily, the inhabitants spoke the same language, albeit with a variety of accents. It was the language of great literature, which non-Italians learned by reading Dante's *Divine Comedy*, the poetry of Petrarch, Tasso, and Ariosto, or by hearing it sung in operas.

MISSION 2

WOLFY REALLY LOVES ITALIAN FOOD. IN FACT, HE OFTEN TALKS ABOUT IT IN HIS BESTSELLER *ITALIAN JOURNEY*! HELP HIM SORT OUT SOME OF ITALY'S TYPICAL DISHES. PUT THE NUMBER OF EACH SPECIALITY IN THE BOX NEXT TO THE CITY WHERE IT WAS BORN.

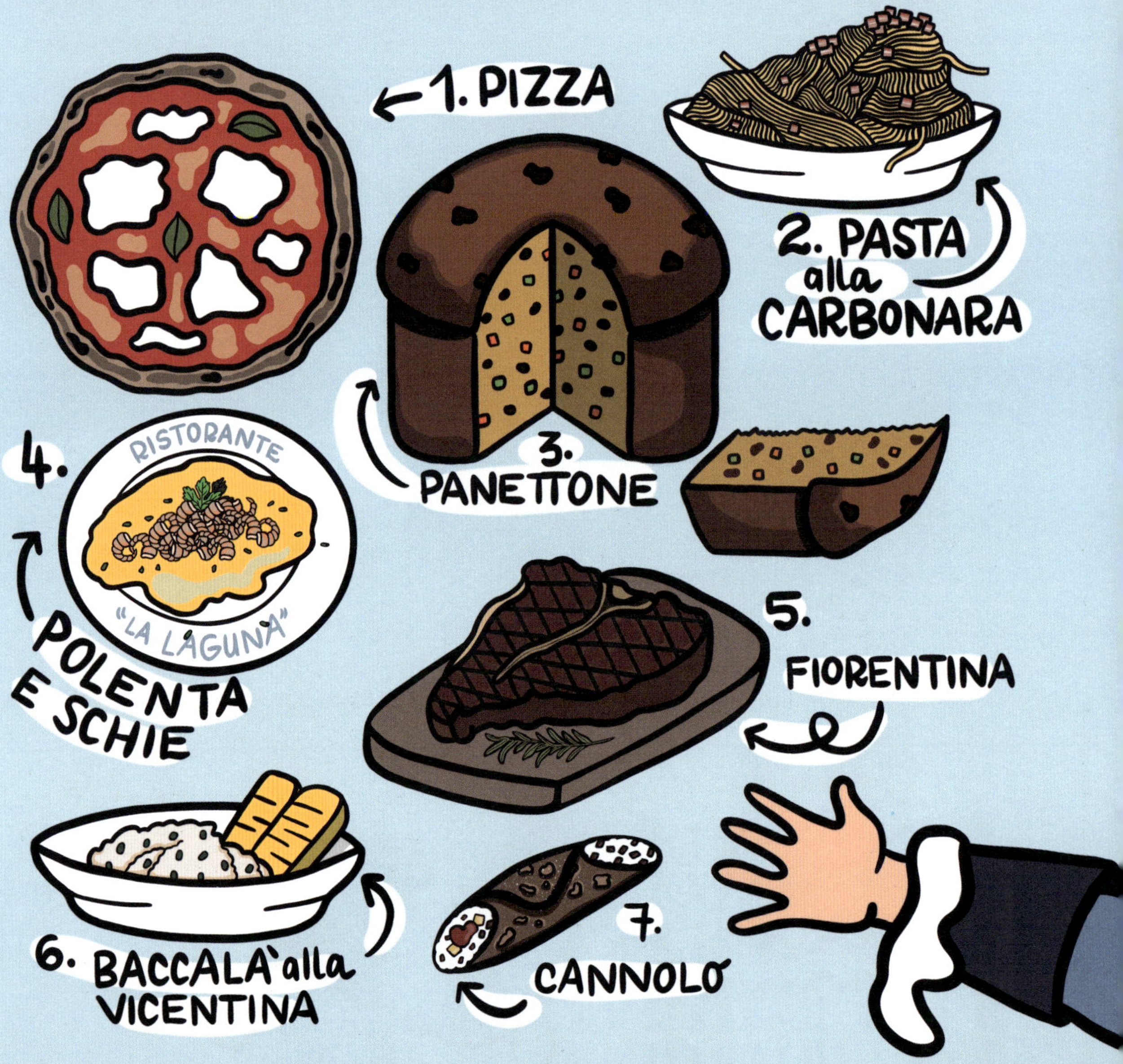
1. PIZZA
2. PASTA alla CARBONARA
3. PANETTONE
4. POLENTA E SCHIE
RISTORANTE "LA LAGUNA"
5. FIORENTINA
6. BACCALÀ alla VICENTINA
7. CANNOLO

ENDORSERS AND INFLUENCERS

Before, during and after their stay in Italy, Grand Tour travellers could consult guides, diaries and in-depth texts available in all languages and covering every necessity. These ranged from booklets with practical information and suggestions to large volumes on art and history. Their authors were writers, philosophers and scholars, and sometimes even ordinary travellers, who described their experiences and gave broad general advice – a bit like Tripadvisor, but centuries before! The most famous among these became major influencers, such as Goethe, the great German poet who was also a renowned scientist and a decent painter, with tens of thousands of followers. His *Italian Journey* was definitely the bestseller among the books dedicated to the Grand Tour. It gives a stage-by-stage account of virtually all of Italy, from the Alps to Sicily, each one filled with descriptions of his personal feelings, adventures, people he met, and the beauty he saw. Goethe was really in love with Italy, and it is also thanks to him that still today many Germans choose Italy for their holidays.

Whereas Goethe returned to Germany at the end of his long journey, another influential German, Johann Winckelmann, settled in Rome, where he methodically and passionately studied archaeology, made friends with painters and sculptors, and concluded that ancient statues are the highest and noblest example of beauty. Winckelmann's writings had such significance that they led to a profound renewal of taste in art known as Neoclassicism, clearly inspired by Greek and Roman antiquity but also influenced by the sensational discoveries of Pompeii and Herculaneum, and the study of the Greek temples in Sicily. Within a short time, and actually due to the purchases, reports, and souvenirs of Grand Tour travellers, this style, which originated in Rome, spread throughout Europe.

MISSION 3

In days gone by, when you visited a beautiful place you sent a postcard to your friends. It was a way of sharing your journey and sending a message. Nowadays we send photos by WhatsApp... Yet postcards were such fun!

draw or glue a picture here

How about sending a postcard from your favourite place in Italy? Draw or glue a picture of your favourite place on the front of the postcard on the left, and write your message on the back below.

THE GENTLEMAN TRAVELLER

Pompeo Batoni, *Portrait of John Staples*, 1773

When travelling, the temptation to take a selfie in front of the most famous monuments is irresistible. Travellers on the Grand Tour in Italy also loved to pose for their portraits next to the artworks they admired.

FRIDGE MAGNETS
(HOW TO MAKE THEM YOURSELF)

✱ WHAT YOU'LL NEED:

- ADHESIVE MAGNETIC SHEETS
- VARIOUS PHOTOS
- SCISSORS
- A PENCIL
- ↳ BONUS: MUM AND DAD's HELP

✱ WHAT YOU MUST DO:

1. PLACE THE PHOTO ON THE MAGNETIC SHEET AND TRACE ITS OUTLINE WITH THE PENCIL.

2. CUT OUT THE SHAPE WITH SCISSORS (<u>BE CAREFUL OR ASK FOR HELP!</u>).

3. WHEN THE SHAPE IS CUT, REMOVE THE ADHESIVE FILM, CAREFULLY POSITION THE PHOTO ON IT AND PRESS IT.

DONE! NOW YOU CAN STICK IT ON THE FRIDGE!

VENICE

Canaletto, *Regatta on the Grand Canal in Venice*, c. 1740

Venice is truly unique in the world, and as such has always stunned travellers. After a lengthy journey by carriage across mountains and plains, they arrived by boat through the still waters of the lagoon, and their amazement was immediate. The ancient city rose spectacularly on a labyrinth of canals, bridges and narrow streets leading up to the solemn square in front of the Basilica of San Marco. Majestic monuments from every period in the most varied styles, and noble palaces of incomparable sumptuousness, formed the backdrop to a city that seemed to be constantly celebrating, populated with masked figures and crowded with gondolas, as if a never-ending carnival was in progress. Sixteen different theatres offered shows of all kinds, as well as comfortable rooms for games and for amorous encounters under the sparkling light of Murano glass chandeliers. Concerts followed one after another, also thanks to the famous orchestra of talented orphans, directed by the musical genius Antonio Vivaldi. For more cultured tourists, the Most Serene City of Venice was also home to masterpieces by artists such as Titian, Giorgione, Tintoretto, and Veronese, and to a remarkable production of paintings depicting the most picturesque views of the city. A veritable master of this genre was Antonio Canal, known throughout Europe by his nickname Canaletto. It was through him that the technique of creating monumental scenes using a camera obscura reached perfection.

Vivaldi's "orphan girls"

MISSION 5

When it's carnival time, Venetians and visiting tourists compete to create the most whimsical and colourful masks.

You can't go to Venice without one!

Unleash your imagination and decorate the mask below with your favourite colours. Use sequins, feathers, fabric scraps, newspaper clippings, glitter, or anything else you like...

... THE SKY IS THE LIMIT!

VICENZA

Francesco Zuccarelli, *Ideal View of Vicenza with the Allegorical Celebration of Andrea Palladio*, c. 1762–65

Who can explain the great monuments of the Italian Renaissance better than the architect who built them? But how is it possible, if the architect in question lived centuries ago? No problem. Andrea Palladio not only designed villas, palaces, churches, and theatres of pure beauty, he also described and illustrated every aspect of these buildings in a book translated into every European language.

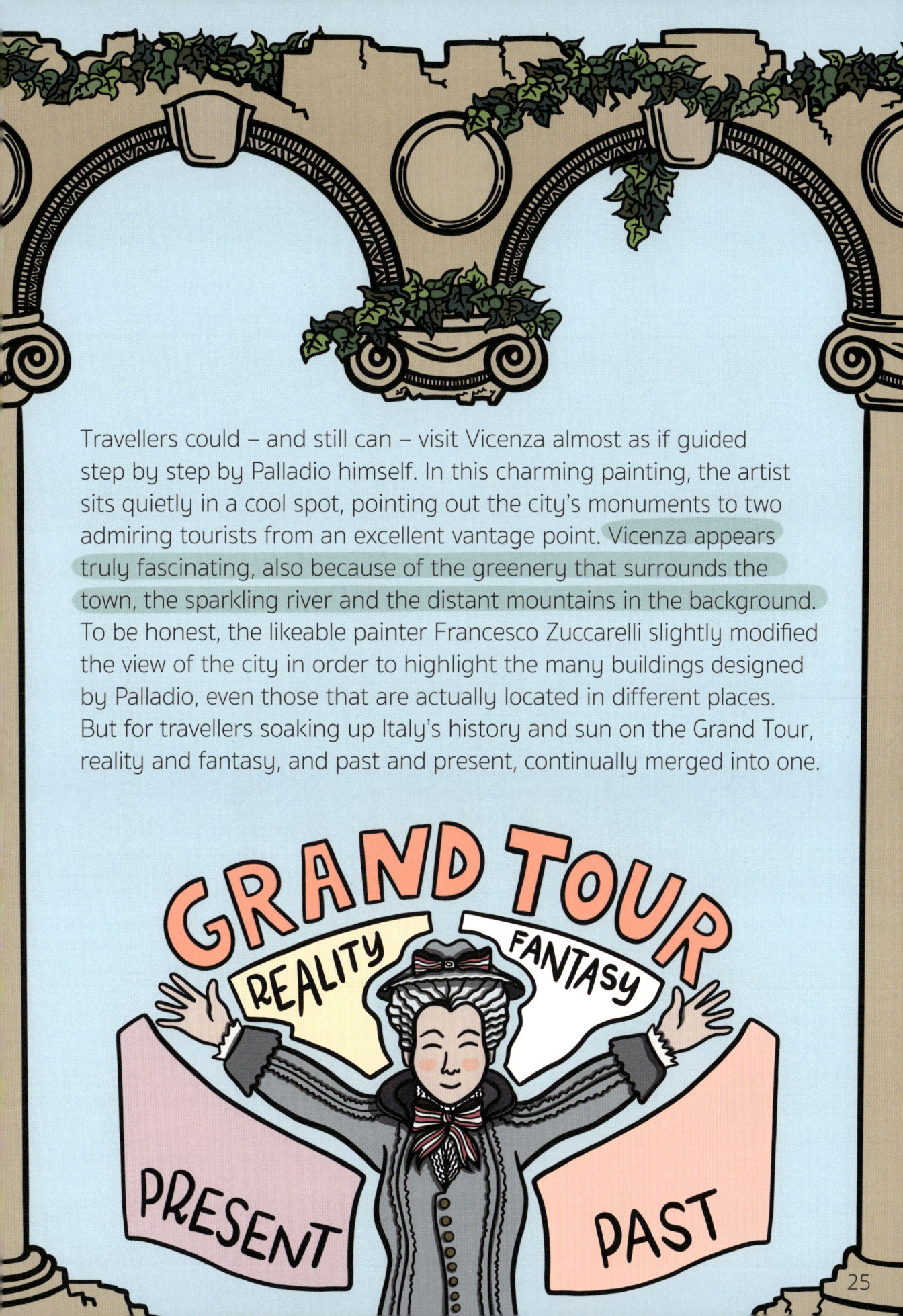

Travellers could – and still can – visit Vicenza almost as if guided step by step by Palladio himself. In this charming painting, the artist sits quietly in a cool spot, pointing out the city's monuments to two admiring tourists from an excellent vantage point. Vicenza appears truly fascinating, also because of the greenery that surrounds the town, the sparkling river and the distant mountains in the background. To be honest, the likeable painter Francesco Zuccarelli slightly modified the view of the city in order to highlight the many buildings designed by Palladio, even those that are actually located in different places. But for travellers soaking up Italy's history and sun on the Grand Tour, reality and fantasy, and past and present, continually merged into one.

MISSION 6

Look out, Palladio got mixed up! He can't find his way among all the villas he's designed. He has to lock four of them before leaving for the next stage. Can you help him?

"OH NO! I HAVE TO LOCK UP BEFORE I LEAVE!"

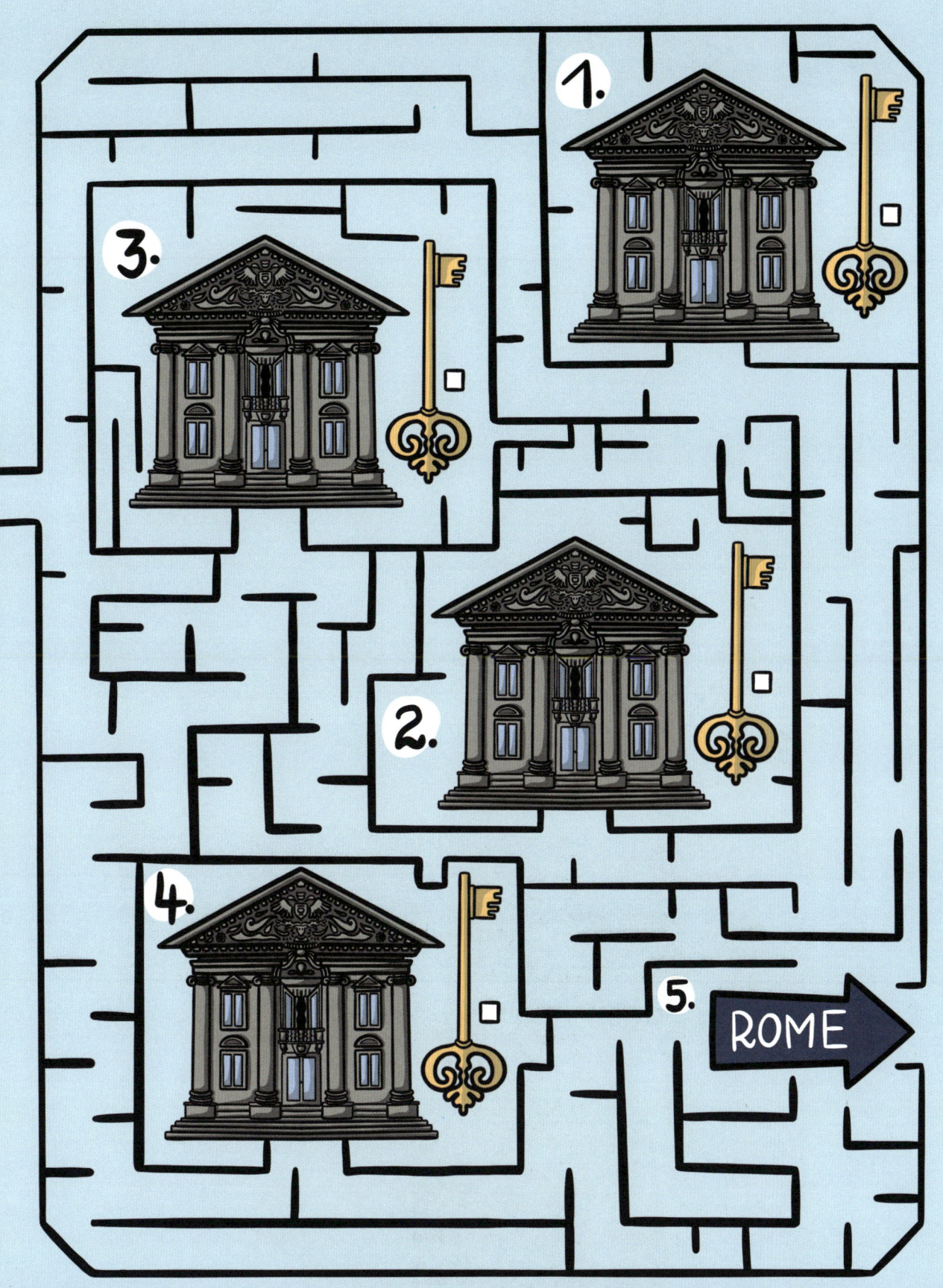

ROME

Gaspar van Wittel, *View of the Colosseum with the Arch of Constantine*, 1716

When Gaspar van Wittel decided to leave the Netherlands to pursue his career as a painter in Italy, he brought with him from Amsterdam a magical and somewhat mysterious box. It was a "camera obscura": a system of lenses and mirrors that enabled painters to observe landscapes, cityscapes and monuments projected onto a sheet of drawing paper. Thus, an artist could follow

their exact lines and reproduce an extremely realistic image, almost like a photograph. The camera obscura was gradually perfected, made portable and easy to operate, becoming an indispensable tool for painters specialising in views, such as the great Venetians Canaletto and Bellotto. Van Wittel was an excellent artist and a dynamic man: he travelled all over Italy, from Venice to Florence and Rome to Naples, confidently selecting the best views and compositions. From then on, many tourists would see Italian cities from exactly the same perspective as the Dutch-born painter. Here, for example, is an unmistakable view of the Colosseum, one of the most famous monuments in the world, rising like a stone giant at the end of the Roman Forum esplanade. Once permanently settled in Italy, van Wittel Italianised his surname to Vanvitelli, and his son Luigi became a famous architect who designed, among other buildings, the Royal Palace of Caserta.

MISSION 7

Welcome travellers to the Eternal City!

my WELCOME TO THE TOWN of
(write its name below)

WHAT TO EXPECT:

WHAT'S THE WEATHER LIKE?

ROME drawn by me

ROME in 3 WORDS:

Offer them valuable advice and suggestions for finding their way around the wonders of Rome. Create a brochure for tourists and colour it!

WONDERS to discover:

*interesting THINGS I FOUND OUT ABOUT ROME:

1. ___
2. ___
3. ___
4. ___
5. ___

SEE WHO LIVES IN ROME:

(IF YOU LIKE, I'LL INTRODUCE YOU)

NAPLES

Pierre-Jacques Volaire, *Eruption of Mount Vesuvius in Moonlight*, after 1774

What a scene! First, Mount Vesuvius rumbles, then it thunders, and finally it erupts fire. During the day a plume of smoke rises from the top of the volcano; at night, fountains of burning lapilli explode as torrents of incandescent lava run down its slopes, illuminating the darkness with frightening yet mesmerising

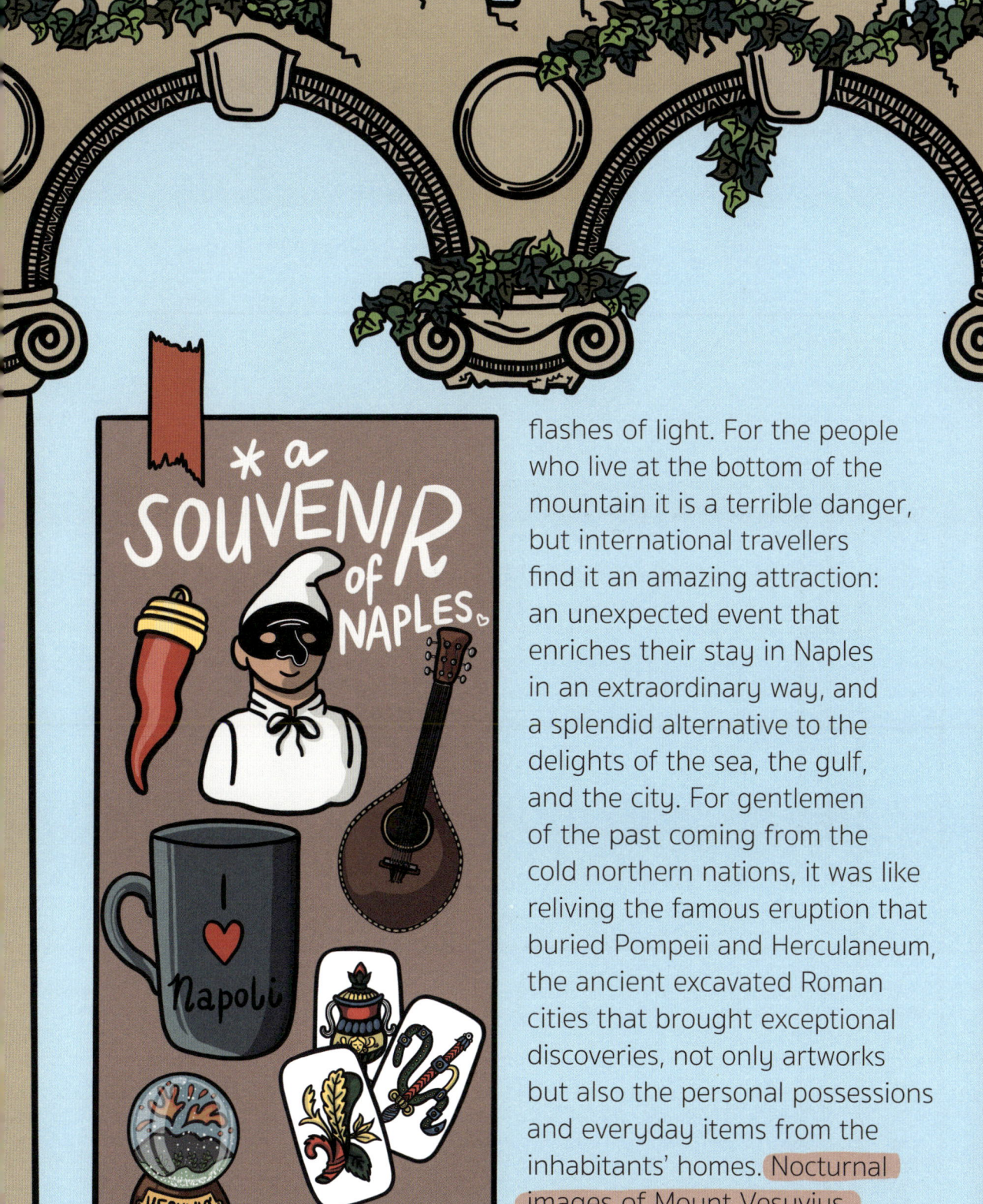

a Souvenir of Naples

flashes of light. For the people who live at the bottom of the mountain it is a terrible danger, but international travellers find it an amazing attraction: an unexpected event that enriches their stay in Naples in an extraordinary way, and a splendid alternative to the delights of the sea, the gulf, and the city. For gentlemen of the past coming from the cold northern nations, it was like reliving the famous eruption that buried Pompeii and Herculaneum, the ancient excavated Roman cities that brought exceptional discoveries, not only artworks but also the personal possessions and everyday items from the inhabitants' homes. Nocturnal images of Mount Vesuvius erupting were amongst the most coveted souvenirs of the Grand Tour, and several painters, such as the French artist Volaire, specialised in this kind of landscape, with its terrifying, almost infernal fascination.

MISSION 8

Some places are so special they become the symbol of a city: a volcano such as Mount Vesuvius, a cathedral or a skyscraper. Artists often portray or photograph their favourite place from different angles. Try it yourself!

10 views of

1.

2.

3.

4.

SICILY

Ferdinand Georg Waldmüller,
The Ruins of the Greek Theatre at Taormina in Sicily, **1844**

For tourists, the Italian tour began with the sunny views seen from the snowy passes of the Alps, but later... where did it end? Naturally, there were unmissable locations, such as fascinating Venice and cultured Florence. Rome was obviously the principal destination, deserving the most time and attention. But there was also Naples with its splendid gulf, theatrical life, archaeological discoveries, and the teeming vitality of the ancient city below the slopes of Vesuvius. But continuing further south there was still a lot of Italy to discover. Travellers who had more time at their disposal journeyed on towards Sicily (part of the Kingdom of Naples and also reachable by sea), attracted primarily by the climate and nature.

Under the Mediterranean light, the island revealed to its visitors from faraway nations the scenery of ancient myths, such as the rocks that rise from the sea facing Aci Trezza, said to be the stones that the Cyclops Polyphemus threw at Ulysses' ship. Or the immense volcano Etna, reputedly the place where the fire god Hephaestus had his foundry. Sicily featured extraordinary archaeological sites of Greek origin, traces of its ancient populations, and architectural masterpieces. Sicily was an intact and, up till then, little-known wonder destined to leave a deep impression on visitors who ventured to this extreme, beautiful boundary of Italy.

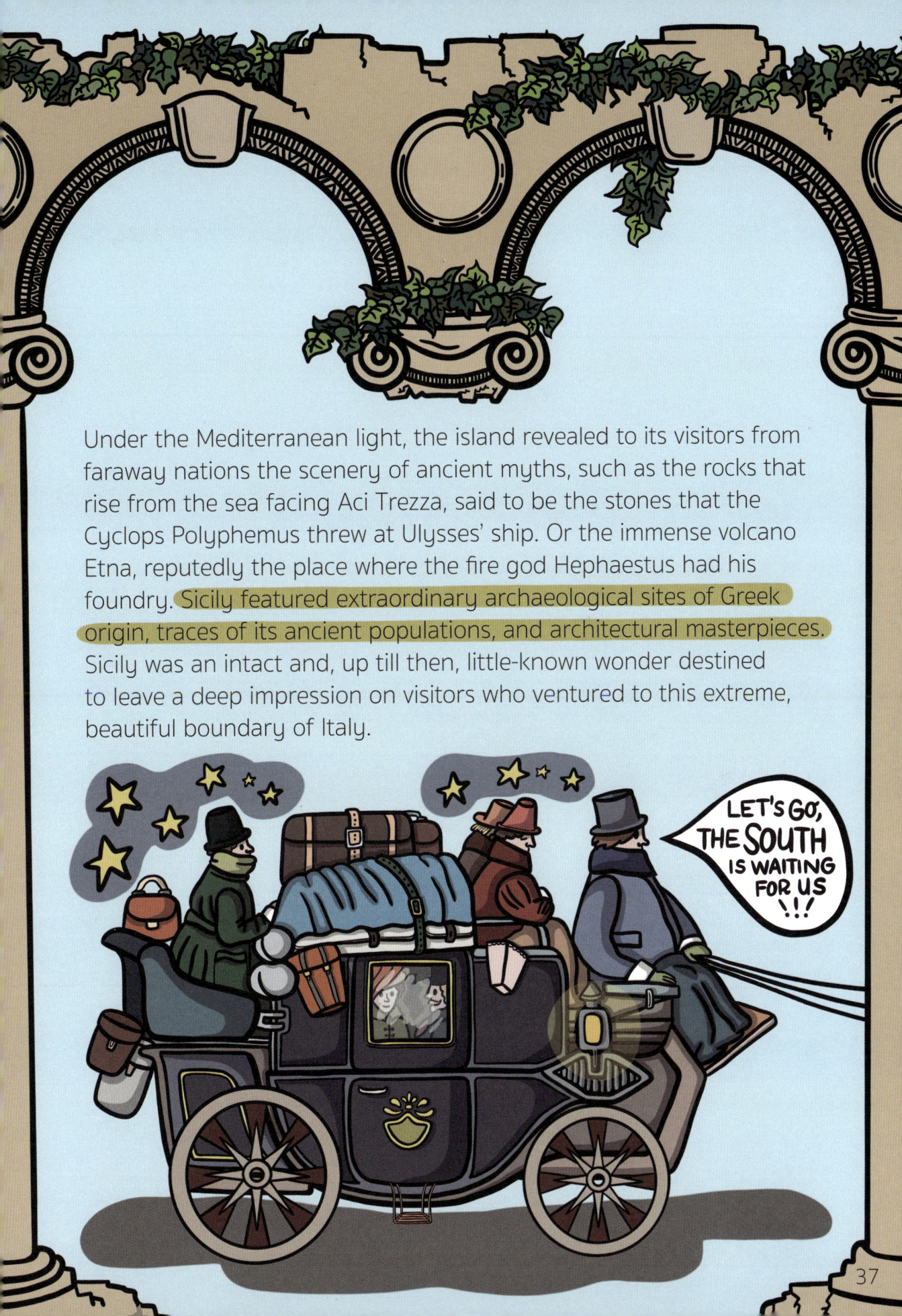

LET'S GO, THE SOUTH IS WAITING FOR US !!!

MISSION 9

They say there was a theatre in every city in Sicily. The remains of wonderful Greek theatres have been preserved for over 2,000 years. Rebuild the one below starting from its ruins. You can also stage a performance and draw the spectators.

FEMALE ARTIST

Louise-Élisabeth Vigée-Le Brun, *Self-Portrait*, 1800

Along the routes of the Grand Tour, many were the fascinating women who could be met: masked Venetian ladies, haughty Roman aristocrats, country girls, the queen, the princesses and their ladies-in-waiting in Naples, pretty maids, famous and majestic opera singers, ambassadors' wives, dancers and female collectors... A special place, however, should be given to female painters.

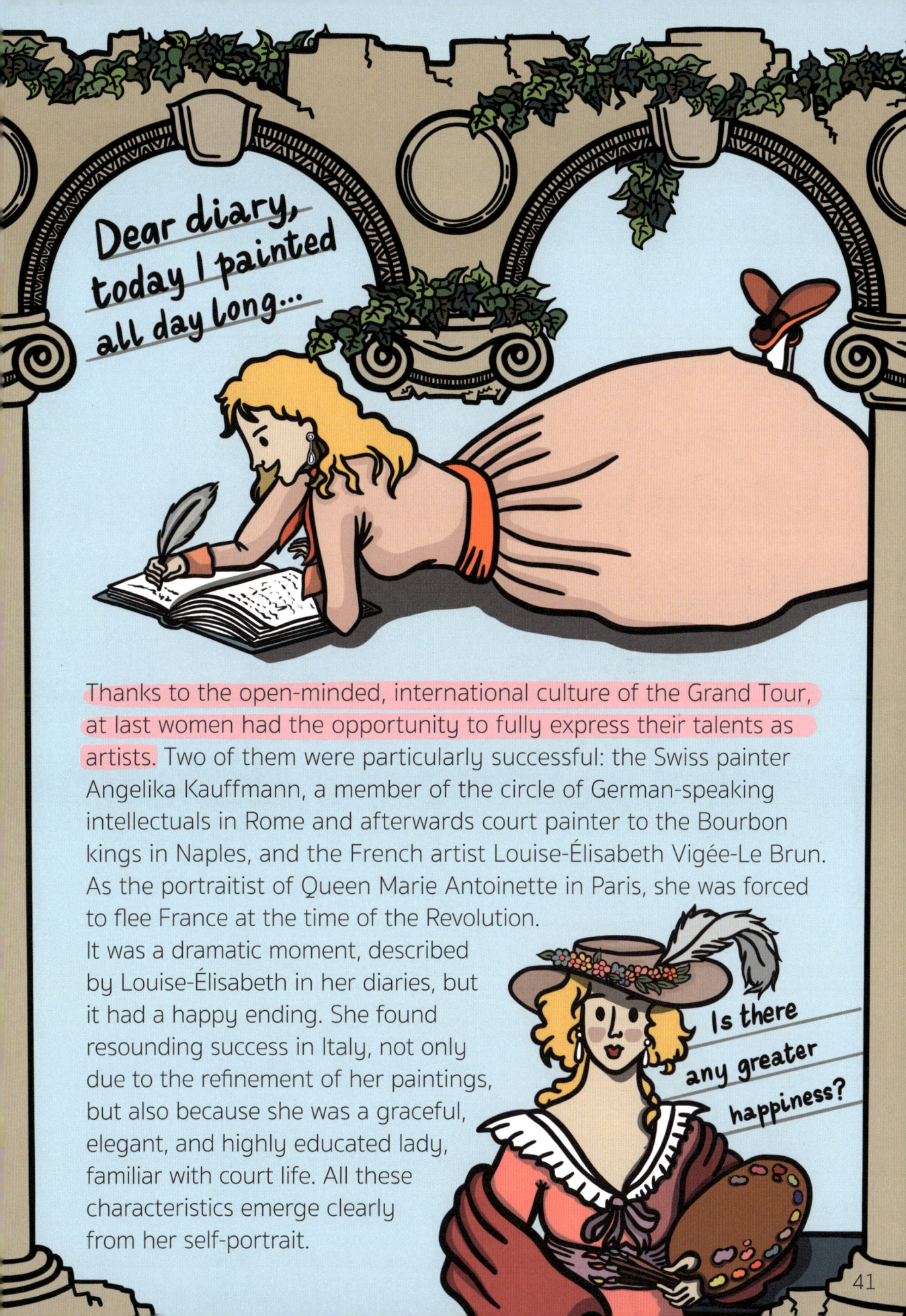

Dear diary, today I painted all day long…

Thanks to the open-minded, international culture of the Grand Tour, at last women had the opportunity to fully express their talents as artists. Two of them were particularly successful: the Swiss painter Angelika Kauffmann, a member of the circle of German-speaking intellectuals in Rome and afterwards court painter to the Bourbon kings in Naples, and the French artist Louise-Élisabeth Vigée-Le Brun. As the portraitist of Queen Marie Antoinette in Paris, she was forced to flee France at the time of the Revolution. It was a dramatic moment, described by Louise-Élisabeth in her diaries, but it had a happy ending. She found resounding success in Italy, not only due to the refinement of her paintings, but also because she was a graceful, elegant, and highly educated lady, familiar with court life. All these characteristics emerge clearly from her self-portrait.

Is there any greater happiness?

"A room with a view"

For travellers of that time, the Grand Tour was also a journey of self-discovery, as perhaps all journeys are. We return from them a little different and also a little happier, because of the things we've seen, the experiences we've had, and the people we've met.
Look through the window-frame on the opposite page. Frame the wonders you see and discover unmissable details of the world around you. Whether you experience it in your own town or on holiday, every trip is a window on the world!

INSTRUCTIONS:

1. Cut out the window on the opposite page (including the inner part along the dashed lines)
2. Choose your view
3. Use the cut-out window to frame it, then take your photo
4. Print your picture
5. You can glue it onto page 47 or hang it in your bedroom!

glue your "Room with a view" here!

captions

Pompeo Batoni, *Portrait of John Staples*, 1773, oil on canvas, 264 × 198 cm, Rome, Museo di Rome (p. 16)

Giovanni Antonio Canal, known as Canaletto, *Regatta on the Grand Canal in Venice*, c. 1740, oil on canvas, 117.2 × 186.7 cm, London, The National Gallery (p. 20)

Francesco Zuccarelli, *Ideal View of Vicenza with the Allegorical Celebration of Andrea Palladio*, c. 1762–65, oil on canvas, 151.5 × 239.5 cm, Intesa Sanpaolo Collection, Vicenza, Gallerie d' Italia – Palazzo Leoni Montanari (p. 24)

Gaspar van Wittel known as Gaspare Vanvitelli, *View of the Colosseum with the Arch of Constantine*, 1716, oil on canvas, 54.6 × 114.3 cm, Norfolk, The Earl of Leicester and the Trustees of the Holkham Estate (p. 28)

Pierre-Jacques Volaire, *Eruption of Mount Vesuvius in Moonlight*, after 1774, oil on canvas, 260 × 385 cm, Maisons-Laffitte, Centre des monuments nationaux, Château de Maisons (p. 32)

Ferdinand Georg Waldmüller, *The Ruins of the Greek Theatre at Taormina in Sicily*, 1844, oil on canvas, 38 × 60 cm, Liechtenstein. The Princely Collections, Vaduz-Vienna (p. 36)

Louise-Élisabeth Vigée-Le Brun, *Self-Portrait*, 1800, oil on canvas, 78.5 × 68 cm, St Petersburg, State Hermitage Museum (p. 40)

credits

© 2021. LIECHTENSTEIN, The Princely Collections, Vaduz-Vienna/SCALA, Florence: p. 36

© Reproduction Patrick Cadet/CMN: p. 32

© Roma- Sovrintendenza Capitolina ai Beni Culturali, Museo di Roma: p. 16

© The National Gallery, London: p. 20

Archivio Patrimonio Artistico Intesa Sanpaolo/foto Valter Maino, Vicenza: p. 24

Bridgeman Images: p. 28

Photograph © The State Hermitage Museum, 2021: p. 40